# A Woman's Prayers of HOPE

Publications International, Ltd.

Interior art from Shutterstock.com.

Scripture quotations from *The Holy Bible, King James Version.*


Louis Weber, CEO
Publications International, Ltd.
7373 North Cicero Avenue
Lincolnwood, Illinois 60712



ISBN: 978-1-68022-321-7

Manufactured in China.

8 7 6 5 4 3 2 1

# Prayers of Hope

Hope is one of God's greatest gifts to us. It keeps dreams alive, no matter how much rejection we face. Hope keeps love alive, no matter how many times our heart breaks. Hope keeps faith alive, for with hope we can have faith in better and brighter times ahead. With such a faith in God, we can keep on going down even the darkest of paths until we find the light up ahead.

We all need hope to put wind in the sails of our lives. *A Woman's Prayers of Hope* is a companion that helps us on our life journey by keeping us filled with God's hope. *A Woman's Prayers of Hope* includes prayers, Bible verses, quotations, and reflections to help keep you hopeful during good times and bad.

**Therefore my heart is glad, and my glory rejoiceth: my flesh also shall rest in hope.**

*—Psalm 16:9*

Like healing waters, hope washes over us and cleanses us of fear, doubt, and worry. The loving presence of God comes to us, showering us with the gentle rain that soothes and strengthens the heart and the spirit. We turn to his light and his love, and our hope is refreshed and renewed.

**Every soul is a melody which needs renewing.**

*—Stephane Mallarme*

**For thou art great, and doest wondrous things: thou art God alone.**

*—Psalm 86:10*

My Creator, blessed is your presence. For you and you alone give me power to walk through dark valleys into the light again. You and you alone give me hope when there seems no end to my suffering. You and you alone give me peace when the noise of my life overwhelms me. I ask that you give this same power, hope, and peace to all who know discouragement, that they, too, may be emboldened and renewed by your everlasting love. Amen.

**The Lord shall preserve thy going out and thy coming in from this time forth, and even for evermore.**

*—Psalm 121:8*

Some women carry pepper spray, some women have a big dog, and some women have taken self-defense classes. There's nothing wrong with being prepared, but ultimately we are not in control of everything that happens to us—no matter how prepared we are. So here we are, vulnerable people in an often-dangerous world. How do we keep from worrying about worst-case scenarios? Only by remembering Psalm 121. God's watch over our lives is continual. We can call out to him for help at all times. So even as you do your best to be safe today, be at peace. God is watching over you.

**Beloved, thou doest faithfully whatsoever thou doest to the brethren, and to strangers. We therefore ought to receive such, that we might be fellowhelpers to the truth.**

*—3 John 1:5, 8*

Galvanize me into prevention, intervention, and rebuilding your world, Creator God. Kids need fixers, not just worriers and those prone to panic. They need to hear plans, not just alarms. Let hope, not fear, be the last word in the bedtime stories I tell.

**There is no hope unmingled with fear, and no fear unmingled with hope.**

*—Baruch de Spinoza*

Put your hope in me, says God, and rejoice in the knowledge that I am working for you 24/7. Put your love on me, says God, and be at peace knowing you are always loved in return. Put your burdens upon me, says God, and rest in the understanding that all will be well. For I am your hope, your peace, and your solution to every challenge. I am your Father, and you are my beloved child.

**But let us, who are of the day, be sober, putting on the breastplate of faith and love; and for an helmet, the hope of salvation.**

*—1 Thessalonians 5:8*

Lord, you are my only hope. When all others fail me, I know I can always turn to you for the love and guidance I need. I thank you for your abiding belief in me, and I cherish the promise of your presence and the miracles you have brought into my life. You alone are my hope and my rock. You alone are my comfort. Thank you, Lord.

**Hope is knowing that no matter how bad "all this" seems, God is still all good.**

We have all felt hopeless at one time or another. It is at those times that life has beaten us down and has robbed us of our will to go on. Yet, somewhere deep inside is a flame—a flame that flickers but never goes out, no matter how strong the winds of despair blow against it. That is the flame of hope, which God has instilled in each of us who understands that this, too, shall pass and that if we but hold on a little longer, things will get better.

Lord, maybe it's in the times we aren't sure that you are hearing our prayers that we learn to trust you the most. Eventually—in your time—we hear your answer. We know that you are still sovereign, and all our hopes and dreams are safe in your hands. Even when the answer to a prayer is "no," we are comforted by the knowledge that you care about us and respond to our concerns in a way that will ultimately be for our good.

**And they that know thy name will put their trust in thee: for thou, Lord, hast not forsaken them that seek thee.**

*—Psalm 9:10*

As I trust in you, God, I know you will fill my life with your hope. That hope will transcend into every area of my soul, and beautiful buds of joy and peace will begin to grow. I want your joy and peace to be obvious in my life. I'm tired of pretending to be joyful and acting like I'm peaceful. I desire those fruits to grow naturally, out of the wellspring of hope in my heart.

Prod me to trust you at all times, Lord, and to rely on your Word. I know that my joy and peace are complete in you, and I have hope that you can work in me despite my weaknesses. I'm done with putting my hope into the changing tides of this world. I'm ready to put all of my hope in you, so real fruits of joy and peace can grow.

**Let us hold fast the profession of our faith without wavering; (for he is faithful that promised).**

*—Hebrews 10:23*

Almighty God, I know you are supremely faithful! Today I ask you to restore hope to the hopeless. Plant seeds of hope in hearts that have lain fallow for so long. Send down showers of hope on those struggling with illness, persecution, or difficult relationships. Hope that comes from you is hope with the power to sustain us when nothing around us seems the least bit hopeful.

**Knowing the source of all hope, may we never be found hopeless.**

**They that sow in tears shall reap in joy.**

*—Psalm 126:5*

O Lord, some days it seems that every hour is spent in toil with little time left over for relaxing with loved ones. Help us keep in mind that our hours of work sow seeds of hope. In time, you will comfort us and restore us to a posture of joy and celebration. Thank you, Lord, for understanding both our need to work hard and our need to enjoy this beautiful life.

**Just a tiny seed of faith, watered with love, wisdom, and hard work, grows into a majestic tree of blessings.**

**Hope is like the sun, which, as we journey towards it, casts the shadow of our burden behind us.**

*—Samuel Smiles*

**Thou art my hiding place and my shield: I hope in thy word.**

*—Psalm 119:114*

As storm clouds gathered, Father, I used to run for cover, panicked and picking a favorite escape. None of them worked for long, dear God, and none of them kept me safe. No more running then. I see it clearly now: Wherever I am standing is a special place, under the shadow of your sheltering wing.

Lord, help me understand that the challenges I am going through serve to empower me. Teach me the wisdom to discern that my trials mold me into something far grander than even I could have imagined. Amen.

**When a determined woman encounters stumbling blocks in her path, she uses them as stepping stones to move closer to the good in life.**

Lord, give me hope,
Give me patience to cope
And a reason to keep on trying.
Take my trembling hand,
Give me power to stand
And a faith that is strong and undying.

Almighty Father, so many people in this world feel completely hopeless. The jobless feel hopeless. The homeless feel hopeless. The unpopular teenager feels hopeless. The overwhelmed mother feels hopeless. Today, loving Father, present yourself to them so they can readily see the source of all hope. Shine a light on each situation, dear Father—a light that casts out the darkness of hopelessness! For there is no such thing as hopelessness in your presence. Amen.

**However long the night,**
**the dawn will break.**

*—African Proverb*

**If any of you lack wisdom, let him ask of God, that giveth to all men liberally, and upbraideth not; and it shall be given him.**

*—James 1:5*

Lord, hope and optimism are gifts from your hand that can guide me for life. When I struggle to hold hope in my heart, please remind me of it. When I batten down the hatches and prepare for the worst, please let me see that there is a new life around the corner for me. When I can't tap into my own wisdom, please lend me yours. Amen.

**There be no potion so powerful, no pill so amazing, and no promised reward so alluring as the certain belief that something good can happen tomorrow.**

**Have not I commanded thee?
Be strong and of a good courage;
be not afraid, neither be thou dismayed:
for the Lord thy God is with thee
whithersoever thou goest.**

*—Joshua 1:9*

**To every thing there is a season, and a time to every purpose under the heaven: A time to be born, and a time to die; a time to plant, and a time to pluck up that which is planted.**

—*Ecclesiastes 3:1–2*

There are few things in life more heartbreaking than the death of a child—one so recently born, exiting life far too soon for our hearts to handle it. There is a time to be born, and a time to die. But there's supposed to be lots of time in between—a lifetime, in fact. How do we pick up the pieces and go on when our hearts ache as they never have before?

O Lord, it is so hard to see the hope in certain circumstances. I guess we just need time. Time to grieve. Time to regain our balance. Time to renew our trust and hope for the future. While we are going through this season of healing, please hold us close.

**And the mother gave, in tears and pain,**
**The flowers she most did love;**
**She knew she should find them all again**
**In the fields of light above.**

*—Henry Wadsworth Longfellow*

**Why art thou cast down, O my soul? and why art thou disquieted in me? hope thou in God: for I shall yet praise him for the help of his countenance.**

*—Psalm 42:5*

Many times I feel that I have the right to be downcast. But God's Word says that we should not be downcast because we have an amazing hope through him. If I focus on this hope, joy will enter my spirit, and my negative emotions will disperse.

**It is good to embrace a hope.**

*—Ovid*

**And Jesus looking upon them saith, With men it is impossible, but not with God: for with God all things are possible.**

*—Mark 10:27*

Lord, how hard it is for us all to live in peace with one another. We all have our own ideas about how the world should be, and some topics can be polarizing. Help us to act in loving ways and to work hard to see and respect others' points of view. We all love this world and you—please help us keep this in mind and work from there. It is easy to get ahead of ourselves and lose hope; we also know, though, that you are always present, and we truly believe that anything is possible with you. We place the troubles of our world at your feet. We know you will mold them into something breathtaking.

**Lord, make me an instrument of your peace,**
**where there is hatred, let me sow love;**
**where there is injury, pardon;**
**where there is doubt, faith...**

*—St. Francis of Assisi*

**For the hope which is laid up for you in heaven, whereof ye heard before in the word of the truth of the gospel.**

*—Colossians 1:5*

**Sometimes, I think, the things we see**
**Are shadows of the things to be;**
**That what we plan we build;**
**That every hope that hath been crossed,**
**And every dream we thought was lost,**
**In heaven shall be fulfilled.**

*—Phoebe Cary*

**The Lord is my shepherd; I shall not want. He maketh me to lie down in green pastures: he leadeth me beside the still waters.**

*—Psalm 23:1–2*

Lord, bring me to the place where peace flows like a river, where soft green grasses gently hold the weight of my tired body, where the light of a new sunrise casts warmth.

**I believe in some blending of hope and sunshine sweetening the worse lots. I believe that this life is not all; neither the beginning nor the end. I believe while I tremble; I trust while I weep.**

*—Charlotte Brontë*

**There is in the worst of fortune the best chances for a happy change**

*—Euripides*

**Therefore if any man be in Christ, he is a new creature: old things are passed away; behold, all things are become new.**

*—2 Corinthians 5:17*

Change is never easy, but the blessings it bestows upon us are magnificent. Just ask the caterpillar struggling within the tight confines of a cocoon. Even as it struggles, it is becoming something glorious, something beautiful, soon to emerge as a winged butterfly. Change may bring temporary pain and discomfort, but it also brings the promise of a new life filled with joy and freedom and the ability to soar even higher than we ever did before.

Some people feel guilty for resorting to prayers of desperation. But God never turns away anyone who sincerely turns to him for help. Even when we've been distant, not walking close to him, he doesn't despise our cries for help as we look to get in step with him again.

**You need not cry very loud:**
**he is nearer to us than we think.**

*—Brother Lawrence*

**For thou art my lamp, O Lord: and the Lord will lighten my darkness.**

*—2 Samuel 22:29*

Jesus is the light of the world. While Christ's followers are called to be lights in a dark world, they don't have to create their own light. Their source is Christ himself. "I am the light of the world," Jesus said. "He that followeth me shall not walk in darkness, but shall have the light of life" (John 8:12). As you go through your days, weeks, months, and years, the Lord himself sheds his light from within you. No matter how thick the darkness may become as it presses against you, the darkness will never overcome you.

**And now, Lord, what wait I for? my hope is in thee. Deliver me from all my transgressions: make me not the reproach of the foolish.**

*—Psalm 39:7–8*

Here we are again, Lord. Another time when I feel like I've made a complete mess of this life you've given me. I place myself in your hands. If you need to totally reshape me to turn me into someone more useful, so be it! Thank you for not abandoning me, your humble creation. Make me over in your design.

**Our Lord Jesus Christ himself, and God, even our Father, which hath loved us, and hath given us everlasting consolation and good hope through grace, Comfort your hearts, and stablish you in every good word and work.**

*—2 Thessalonians 2:16–17*

Sometimes the circumstances of our lives are so difficult, Lord! Often misfortunes seem to come all at once. Other times ongoing, wear-me-down situations or relationships seem to follow us day in and day out. Then there are the crushing tragedies that strike us in our tracks and devastate us. A life of faith is not defined by these things—but it is not exempt, either. Suffering is as real for the faithful as for anyone else. However, we have an "everlasting consolation and good hope" that lifts us up. In that comfort and hope, God carries us, heals us with the balm of his tender mercies, and strengthens us to carry on.

**Regardless of circumstances today, may you keep the faith within the hope and comfort of Christ's eternal love for you.**

**I will lift up mine eyes unto the hills, from whence cometh my help. My help cometh from the Lord.**

*—Psalm 121:1–2*

Lord, today I pray for all those who are in desperate need of help in order to survive: victims of earthquakes and tornadoes, the homeless, and the physically and emotionally destitute people of our world. Make yourself known to them, Lord. May they all see that their true help and hope comes only from you! You who created them will not leave them without help, nor without hope.

**Without Christ there is no hope.**

*—Charles Spurgeon*

**And thou shalt be secure, because there is hope; yea, thou shalt dig about thee, and thou shalt take thy rest in safety.**

*—Job 11:18*

We often think of security as having enough money to retire, or a good enough salary to pay for a home. We only feel safe when we are shored up in our homes with alarms, protected from the outside world. Yet putting our hope in material things will never truly give us a deep and abiding peace. Only putting our hope in God will do that. Hope in him is our ultimate security and our eternal protection.

**What is the secret to long-term security? Trust in God.**

Hope uplifts us. Hope carries us when we are too tired to walk on our own. Hope inspires us, motivates us, and encourages us. Even as we stand in shadows, hope reminds us of the warmth of the sun once the clouds drift away. Even as we mourn in sorrow, hope heals us with promises of a future filled with love, happiness, and laughter. Hope keeps us afloat when the weight of the world threatens to sink us.

**A single sunbeam is enough to drive away many shadows.**

*—St. Francis of Assisi*

**Children are the hands by which we take hold of heaven.**

*—Henry Ward Beecher*

Children hope without question, and dream without limitation. When we come to God in childlike awe and wonder, he fulfills all our hopes and dreams beyond our wildest imaginings. The open heart of a child is like a door through which God can easily enter and do his will. Be as a child again. Open your heart. Hope. Dream. No questions. No limitations.

**Blessed is the man that trusteth in the Lord, and whose hope the Lord is.**

*—Jeremiah 17:7*

It's fine to hope for things. We may not always get what we hoped for, but chances are we will get something even better, or find out we didn't really need what we thought we had to have. When we make the Lord our hope, we always get the best of everything, every time. Hope for his presence, and all else will fall into place.

**God will either give you what you ask, or something far better.**

*—Robert Murray McCheyne*

There are times when we might feel as if we've messed things up in life beyond all hope. But God is in the business of redemption—of taking messed up situations and people and restoring them. It's like those home makeover shows where they transform an unlivable space into a lovely habitation. "We know that all things work together for good to them that love God," Paul assures us, "to them who are the called according to his purpose" (Romans 8:28). There's always hope when God is in the house.

It has been said in jest, "Never pray for patience!" The joke is that doing so would invite all sorts of trials for working the desired quality into our character. Fortunately, there's a better way to grow in patience. God's Spirit cultivates true patience in our hearts, helping us become "swift to hear, slow to speak, slow to wrath" (James 1:19). We also learn to wait for God's direction instead of running ahead on our own. The net result: less stress all the way around.

Lord, on days when everything seems to go wrong, help me to remember that you are always nearby to offer comfort. It is easy to get overwhelmed and feel lost and alone in this world, but deep down I know that is never the case. You are always at the ready to help—I just need to remember to take a moment to stop, breathe, and pray.

**Hope knows that in the midst of feeling all alone, God is still with me.**

**Wherefore gird up the loins of your mind, be sober, and hope to the end for the grace that is to be brought unto you at the revelation of Jesus Christ.**

*—1 Peter 1:13*

Knowing God is our source of all love, comfort, and strength allows us to keep our hope alive, no matter what might be going on around us. The world can be a scary place, but we have the revelation of God's love for us to hold onto. We have hope as our anchor to him to keep us safe from the stormy seas of life.

**And there is hope in thine end, saith the Lord, that thy children shall come again to their own border.**

*—Jeremiah 31:17*

Sometimes our parents have hopes for themselves that they may not live long enough to see come to fruition. But they continue to hope and to work hard, because they know that their children will be the beneficiaries of the fruits of their labors, and their faith and trust in God. They pay hope forward, blessing the generations to come.

**In self-doubting times, we can rely on God as a loving parent who wills wholeness for each of his children.**

Dear Father, I come to you in prayer, asking that you open my heart to the hope of better days ahead. Life is hard, and times are tough in the world, but my hope is all I have sometimes to keep me from giving up. I seek your continued grace as I face any challenges, that I may best do your will, even when things seem close to the breaking point. Help me to stay centered in hope, and not fear, as I move about in the world. Amen.

**When you get into a tight place and it seems you can't go on, hold on, for that's just the place and time that the tide will turn.**

*—Harriet Beecher Stowe*

**For we are saved by hope: but hope that is seen is not hope: for what a man seeth, why doth he yet hope for?**

*—Romans 8:24*

Imagine only having hope for things you already can see and hold in your hands? That is not hope at all. Hope is the promise of the unseen, but desired outcome. To have hope means to be strong enough in mind and spirit to suspend our reliance on the seen, and believe in the yet-to-be-seen.

**All I have seen teaches me to trust the Creator for all I have not seen.**

*—Ralph Waldo Emerson*

**And I will bring the blind by a way that they knew not; I will lead them in paths that they have not known: I will make darkness light before them, and crooked things straight. These things will I do unto them, and not forsake them.**

*—Isaiah 42:16*

When the road into the future looms endlessly dark, remember ancient desert nomads who only traveled in the dark because of the heat during the day. They sewed tiny candleholders on their shoes so they always had enough light for the next step. God is both our light in the darkness and the ingenuity to use it.

**The Lord is my portion, saith my soul; therefore will I hope in him.**

*—Lamentations 3:24*

Like food for the soul, hope satisfies our deepest needs. Like water for a thirsty spirit, hope quenches us. Like shelter for a cold and tired body, hope covers us with wings and warms us. Hope is the gift of God's nourishment and the blessing of his comfort that keeps us alive, thriving, and happy.

**Hope is the lone flower blooming in times of life's desert.**

Lord, what comfort we find in your changeless nature. When we look back and remember all the ways you've guided us in the past, we know we have no need to be anxious about the future. You were, are, and always will be our Savior and Lord. Why should we fear instability when you are always here with us?

**Earth changes, but thy soul and God stand sure.**

*—Robert Browning*

**Be not far from me; for trouble is near; for there is none to help.**

*—Psalm 22:11*

God of hope, keep me close today. I am not at my best, and I would like someone to listen as I whine, moan, and complain. Please bear the brunt of my troubles or send someone to help in your name. Amen.

Our hope is in God's promises. When we tell others about our faith, we point to God's promises: his promise to forgive us if we confess our sin; his promise to save us if we'll trust in Christ; his promise to give us eternal life; his promise to never leave us; and his promise to return. Hebrews 10:23 proclaims, "Let us hold fast the profession of our faith without wavering; (for he is faithful that promised)." God wants us to know that if our hope is firmly set on his promises, he will fulfill them.

**Jesus said unto them, Because of your unbelief: for verily I say unto you, If ye have faith as a grain of mustard seed, ye shall say unto this mountain, Remove hence to yonder place; and it shall remove; and nothing shall be impossible unto you.**

*—Matthew 17:20*

Jesus encourages us to have faith, to trust a little deeper, and to have the confidence that with God all things are possible. A seemingly insurmountable and impossible challenge, like moving mountains, can be overcome by even a little mustard seed of faith.

**He who trusts himself is lost.**
**He who trusts in God can do all things.**

*—Alphonsus Liguori*

**And every man that hath this hope in him purifieth himself, even as he is pure.**

*—1 John 3:3*

A heart that is pure of motive and intent is a heart that hopes, and, having hoped, finds joy and peace. That is what our God does for us when we put our hopes in his power and his will for us. His motives and intents are always for our highest good, and when we surrender to his plan, our hopes are made manifest.

**But it is good for me to draw near to God:
I have put my trust in the Lord God,
that I may declare all thy works.**

*—Psalm 73:28*

I put my hopes in the Lord, that he may fulfill them in due time. I take my strength from the Lord, that he may carry me when I am too weak to walk on my own.

**Continue patiently, believingly, perseveringly to wait upon God.**

*—George Muller*

**For there is hope of a tree, if it be cut down, that it will sprout again, and that the tender branch thereof will not cease.**

*—Job 14:7*

Proper respect pleases God. "He delighteth not in the strength of the horse: he taketh not pleasure in the legs of a man. The Lord taketh pleasure in them that fear him, in those that hope in his mercy" (Psalm 147:10–11). While things like strength and speed, fame and fortune may wow the human race, God's value system is more about what's inside us than about what we can accomplish. The kinds of things that make God's heart glad have to do with our trust and hope in him, how we relate to him, and how we show our love in return.

**The hope of the righteous shall be gladness: but the expectation of the wicked shall perish.**

*—Proverbs 10:28*

A hopeful heart does not seek greed or power or glory or attention for itself. It has no material expectations and places no conditions upon God to deliver this or that or satisfy its vanity. It makes no demands or threats to God. A hopeful heart is a righteous heart that gratefully accepts what God offers and rejoices in gladness for it.

Father, make me resilient like the sandy beach upon which the waves crash. Make me strong like the mighty willow tree that bends but does not break in the high winds. Give me the patience and wisdom to know that my suffering will one day turn to a greater understanding of your ways, your works, and your wonders.

**Our real blessings often appear to us in the shape of pains, losses and disappointments; but let us have patience, and we soon shall see them in their proper figures.**

*—Joseph Addison*

**Blessed be God, even the Father of our Lord Jesus Christ, the Father of mercies, and the God of all comfort; Who comforteth us in all our tribulation, that we may be able to comfort them which are in any trouble, by the comfort wherewith we ourselves are comforted of God.**

*—2 Corinthians 1:3–4*

Lord, only you can take all the heartaches and failures in our lives and turn them into compassionate messages of hope for others. We care for an aging parent who passes away, and so are able to relate to the needs of the elderly around us. We go through a divorce, and we can then give genuine advice during our interactions with single mothers. Our pain becomes others' gain, Lord. Sometimes looking back over our shoulders brings us hope for the opportunities that are surely ahead of us. Thank you for second chances.

**I am the good shepherd, and know my sheep, and am known of mine. As the Father knoweth me, even so know I the Father: and I lay down my life for the sheep.**

*—John 10:14–15*

As children we can't wait to grow up. As adults, we often wonder why we were in such a hurry. Taking care of ourselves (and the people who rely on us) is a big job. Wouldn't it be nice to have someone taking care of us again? "I am the good shepherd, and know my sheep," Jesus said. "I lay down my life for the sheep." Jesus offers to be our protector and guardian. He even sacrificed himself to save us. Truly his care for us is like no other.

Dear Lord, each night the news is full of trouble. So much pain and sorrow. It makes me ache to see it all. Some nights, it seems that's all there is; this world seems sometimes so weary and heavy laden.

Then I turn to you and know that you are nearest on the darkest days. And there is comfort in knowing you and that you have not forsaken us.

**And the peace of God, which passeth all understanding, shall keep your hearts and minds through Christ Jesus.**

*—Philippians 4:7*

Moms are powerful purveyors of peacefulness. When a mother is at peace, her child responds more peacefully. Like a ray of sunshine that gives warmth to everything in its path, a mother's harmony gives order to everyone she comes in contact with.

Spirit, help me live one day at a time so that I may meet each day's challenges with grace, courage, and hope. Shelter me from the fears of the future and the anguish of the past. Keep my mind and heart focused on the present, where the true gift of happiness and healing is to be found. Amen.

# Peter's Promise of Hope

**Blessed be the God and Father of our Lord Jesus Christ, which according to his abundant mercy hath begotten us again unto a lively hope by the resurrection of Jesus Christ from the dead. To an inheritance incorruptible, and undefiled, and that fadeth not away, reserved in heaven for you, who are kept by the power of God through faith unto salvation ready to be revealed in the last time, wherein ye greatly rejoice, though now for a season, if need be, ye are in heaviness through manifold temptations.**

*—1 Peter 1:3–6*

O Lord, what a blessing children are in this world. They bring such joy into our lives and are a precious composite of the best of our past and our hopes for the future. Thank you for your love for all children, Lord. Please guard them always.

Even in the direst of situations, we find the courage and resilience to keep moving forward. God's bright and eternal flame of hope lights the way through the darkness. We will never be given more than we can handle, and our hope in God's mercy will always deliver us back into the light again.

**Whatever enlarges hope**
**will also exalt courage.**

*—Samuel Johnson*

**And he saith unto them, Be not affrighted: Ye seek Jesus of Nazareth, which was crucified: he is risen; he is not here: behold the place where they laid him.**

*—Mark 16:6*

Jesus had promised his followers that he would die, and then rise again. Sometimes he spoke in parables, though, and perhaps they thought (or hoped) he was speaking metaphorically. But then on that morning—that mind-blowing morning—when Jesus exited his tomb in triumph over our nemesis death, there was no doubt that he had meant what he had said. "Behold," the angel exclaimed. In other words, "See for yourself that it's true." Jesus has risen, and he opened the way to eternal life for all who trust in him.

**Hope, like the glimmering taper's light,**
**Adorn and cheers our way;**
**And still, as darker grows the night,**
**Emits a brighter ray.**

*—Oliver Goldsmith*

**Commit thy way unto the Lord; trust also in him; and he shall bring it to pass.**

*—Psalm 37:5*

Lord, this is one of those days when I really don't know which way to turn. I've lost my sense of direction and feel as if I'm sitting on a rock in the forest, wondering which trail will take me back to familiar ground. Lead me, Lord. Send the signs I need to follow to get where you want me to go. I put my trust in you.

**Hope writes the poetry of the boy, but memory that of the man. Man looks forward with smiles, but backward with sighs. Such is the wise providence of God. The cup of life is sweetest at the brim—the flavor is impaired as we drink deeper, and the dregs are made bitter that we may not struggle when it is taken from our lips.**

*—Ralph Waldo Emerson*

**Rejoicing in hope; patient in tribulation; continuing instant in prayer.**

*—Romans 12:12*

Lord, sometimes I feel like throwing in the towel. I have so many responsibilities, and it is hard to keep up. Some days I juggle everything flawlessly, but then one of those days comes along. I oversleep, and I rush to drop the kids off at school. I arrive at work late, only to realize we have a meeting with an important client, and I am woefully unprepared. I finally get home after working late, and I am met with the news that one of my children is in trouble at school. I feel like a failure on days like this, Lord. Comfort me and fill me with the hope that only you can give. Give me the strength to keep going even when it's hard, so I can revel in the growth that results.

**Son, be of good cheer;**
**thy sins be forgiven thee.**

*—Matthew 9:2*

Father, the beginning of a new year speaks of a fresh start and new opportunities. It is a good time to teach our children about forgiveness and trying again when we have failed.

We are thankful that you are a God of second chances. Just as you love us unconditionally, there is nothing our children could do to make us stop loving them. Help us teach them the hopeful message that there is no need for despair; that forgiveness and a new start are always possible.

**But let all those that put their trust in thee rejoice: let them ever shout for joy, because thou defendest them: let them also that love thy name be joyful in thee.**

*—Psalm 5:11*

As we learn to trust you, God, we discover your strengthening presence in various places and people. Wherever we encounter shelter, comfort, rest, and peace, we are bound to hear your voice, welcoming us. And in whomever we find truth, love, gentleness, and humility, we are sure to hear your heartbeat, assuring us that you will always be near. Thank you, God.

**And we know that all things work together for good to them that love God, to them who are the called according to his purpose.**

—*Romans 8:28*

Lord, this morning as I was mending a beautiful quilt a friend made for me, I thought again about how all the parts of our lives come together to form something beautiful and useful. Even the mistakes I would love to be able to erase from my memory helped make me who I am today; I'm grateful I've been able to see the good that could come of them. May I always look back without regret and look forward with hope, knowing that when all is said and done my life will have been full—and wonderful.

**Hope opens our hearts**
**And lessens our woes.**
**It fights against strife**
**And vanquishes foes.**
**It can be as small as a smile**
**Or as long as the day.**
**It's a gift that grows larger**
**When you give it away.**

**Happy is he that hath the God of Jacob for his help, whose hope is in the Lord his God.**

*—Psalm 146:5*

The psalmist knew that with and through hope, we could find happiness in this life. Even though the principle of hope is a spiritual one, extending into eternity, it can also sustain us through the everyday challenges of life. We can, through hope, bring the strength of heaven into our homes, our workplaces, our minds, and our hearts.

Our hope in God's promises empowers us with an eternal perspective.

**Be of good courage, and he shall strengthen your heart, all ye that hope in the Lord.**

*—Psalm 31:24*

Lord, let me be strong today, drawing my courage from my hope in you. Help me lean not on my own strength but on your limitless power. I know there is work to be done—burdens to be lifted, temptations to be resisted, and unkindness to be forgiven. Let my thoughts and actions be motivated by the hope generated by your promises.

**And now abideth faith, hope, charity, these three; but the greatest of these is charity.**

*—1 Corinthians 13:13*

It can be tempting to write hope off as weak. We often hear, "I hope it doesn't rain." Using hope in this way is mere wishing with no power behind it. And yet, hope matters. Hope, love, and faith are closely related. Paul listed these specific three for a reason. They are the inseparable sister virtues, each one stronger through association with the other two. A faithful woman is even stronger if she is also a hopeful woman; and the faithful, hopeful woman is all the more complete if she is also a loving woman. When used together, these beautiful qualities multiply their power and result in immense strength.

Lord, sometimes I worry about my loved ones. Though I often complain of the monotony of my day-to-day life, I know my days are full of moments to be treasured. When I hear shocking, horrific stories on the news, I often wonder how I would handle such events if they were to befall me or a loved one. Father, I cling to your promise that you give each of us a future filled with hope. I am grateful that you hear me when I come to you in prayer. Please stay close to me and my loved ones. Grant us the strength to prevail in all circumstances.

**Trust ye in the Lord for ever: for in the Lord Jehovah is everlasting strength.**

*—Isaiah 26:4*

Lord, if we could see the future, it would be easy to have hope. Real hope is when we can't see the end of the road, but still trust you to lead us there.

**But well for him whose feet hath trod**
**The weary road of toil and strife,**
**Yet from the sorrows of his life**
**Builds ladders to be nearer God.**

*—Oscar Wilde, "A Lament"*

**And he believed in the Lord; and he counted it to him for righteousness.**

*—Genesis 15:6*

Today I'll simply trust you, Father. I'll remember that you're not looking for résumés full of impressive credentials; rather, you seek hearts that trust in you. You want to enjoy a vibrant, meaningful relationship with me—a relationship in which I trust you fully. That's the starting point of a life lived for you.

Heavenly Father, there are many events in our lives over which we have no control. However, we do have a choice either to endure trying times or to give up. Remind us that the secret of survival is remembering that our hope is in your fairness, goodness, and justice. When we put our trust in you

who cannot fail us, we can remain faithful. Our trust and faithfulness produce the endurance that sees us through the tough times we all face in this life. Please help us to remember. Amen.

**To whom God would make known what is the riches of the glory of this mystery among the Gentiles; which is Christ in you, the hope of glory.**

*—Colossians 1:27*

O God, how it breaks my heart to see pain and loneliness in someone's eyes. Because of the unfolding of your miraculous plan to send your son to die for us, hopelessness should never take up residence in us, Lord! We can be filled with your Spirit so quickly if we just focus on you. Help me bring your hope to those in despair, Lord.

Lord, lately I really do feel like a tree that has been chopped down. Everything that I've held dear has been taken from me; I feel numb, and my life seems meaningless. Hope seems far away.

I have not forgotten, though, that you are a God of new life. I trust that the sun will shine again and the rain will fall when necessary. It is hard to let go of what was, but I believe that I will grow strong and my heart will again leap for joy rather than merely throb with this dull ache. My roots are secure in you, Lord—I will not allow myself to remain so shaken. Though the storms of this life uproot and tear down, I will hold steadfast to hope.

**For our sakes, no doubt, this is written: that he that ploweth should plow in hope; and that he that thresheth in hope should be partaker of his hope.**

*—1 Corinthians 9:10*

Have you ever seen a farmer plow a field, plant the seeds, and then try to harvest his crop the very next day? No—that would be a pretty silly farmer! Yet sometimes we think we can get a reward or "harvest" without the time and effort it takes to plow, plant, and wait patiently for a crop that is ripe for the harvest. Lord, today I will plant a few seeds, nurture ones I have already planted, and strive to "plow in hope" while I wait for harvest day.

Dear Lord, my financial demands exceed the resources I have. The pressure I feel to do something, even if it's unwise, is building, and I fear I will cave in and make a decision I will regret. Help me trust you. Preserve my integrity and show me your way of dealing with this situation.

**One song can spark a moment,**
**One flower can wake the dream.**
**One tree can start a forest,**
**One bird can herald spring.**
**One smile begins a friendship,**
**One hand clasp lifts a soul.**
**One star can guide a ship at sea,**
**One word can frame the goal.**
**One vote can change a nation,**
**One sunbeam lights a room.**
**One candle wipes out darkness,**
**One laugh will conquer gloom.**

*—Unknown*

**Then she said, Did I desire a son of my lord? did I not say, Do not deceive me?**

*—2 Kings 4:28*

The prophet Elisha wants to do something special for a woman who has continuously blessed his ministry. When he asks what she would like, she tells him that there is nothing she needs. Elisha does a little research and finds that she never had a son; he then tells the woman that she will give birth to a son in one year's time.

Instead of rejoicing, the woman cries in fear. Her hope for a son died long ago, and she is terrified to expose herself to more heartbreak.

The weight of hope can be heavy on our souls, and many times we will want to give up on our dreams. But until our yearnings change or subside, we must keep our hope in God's timing and plans. It's okay to raise our hopes in a God who can perform miracles.

**Truly my soul waiteth upon God: from him cometh my salvation. He only is my rock and my salvation; he is my defence; I shall not be greatly moved.**

—*Psalm 62:1–2*

Lord, today I pray for all those who have sought all the wrong kinds of protection. It's so easy for us to become obsessed with protecting our marriages, our children, and our well-being to the extent that we are in danger of losing our peace of mind. Remind us all, Lord, that when we are in your hands, we are in the best of hands. You will never fail us. You will never renege on your promises. With you, we stand strong and have great hope.

God's Spirit will guide us. All the stress goes out of navigating unknown territory when you have a guide. The guide knows all the best places to go, the shortcuts, the scenic routes, and the places to avoid. For our guide in life, God has given us his Spirit. The unknown future lies before us at every moment, but it is not unknown to God. His Spirit will lead us if we'll accept his guidance. "If we live by the Spirit," Paul said, "let us also walk in the Spirit" (Galatians 5:25).

Thank you, Father, for your Holy Spirit, who guides me through each day. May I willingly follow your lead, no matter the time or place. If I follow your Spirit, I can't go wrong.

**Blessed are they that have not seen, and yet have believed.**

*—John 20:29*

When my children were young, they used to wander away sometimes, and I would have trouble finding them for a few moments. As humans we're prone to say "seeing is believing," and I could never rest until I had the little ones in sight again. But this urge is strictly of the earth. Our greatest gift is our ability to think beyond what we see and imagine the possibilities.

We trust in the Lord to care for us, and he, in turn, trusts in us to care for each other. We can honor his faith in us by pledging to serve our communities. We can truly live his love by caring for our neighbors.

**The wonder of serving is when we meet the needs of others, forgetting about our own, and yet somehow in the process our needs are met.**

**Above all, taking the shield of faith, wherewith ye shall be able to quench all the fiery darts of the wicked.**

*—Ephesians 6:16*

Guide me, O God, as I encourage my loved ones to be positive—to see the good in each day, each person, each challenge. Let them use faith to bolster themselves in a world that can seem random at best. Hope and optimism are gifts from your hand that can guide them for life.

**What woman having ten pieces of silver, if she lose one piece, doth not light a candle, and sweep the house, and seek diligently till she find it? And when she hath found it, she calleth her friends and her neighbours together, saying, Rejoice with me; for I have found the piece which I had lost. Likewise, I say unto you, there is joy in the presence of the angels of God over one sinner that repenteth.**

—*Luke 15:8–10*

These verses fill my heart with hope, Lord. Sometimes—when I'm lost on this path of life—I sense your presence. It is so comforting to think of you searching tirelessly to find me again. Grant me your grace so I can stay on your paths more steadily. This way, you'll have more time to devote to searching out others!

Offering hope to others through a loving word, a thoughtful act, or a simple smile is the surest way to lift your own spirit.

**Ah, Hope! what would life be, stripped of thy encouraging smiles, that teach us to look behind the dark clouds of to-day, for the golden beams that are to gild the morrow.**

*—Susanna Moodie*

**This day is holy unto our Lord: neither be ye sorry; for the joy of the Lord is your strength.**

*—Nehemiah 8:10*

Grace of my heart, I turn to you when I am feeling lost and alone. You restore me with strength and hope and the courage to face a new day. You bless me with joy and comfort me through trials and tribulations. You direct my thoughts, guide my actions, and temper my words. You give me the patience and kindness I need to be good. Grace of my heart, I turn to you. Amen.

**Let me but live my life from year to year,**
**With forward face and unreluctant soul;**
**Not hurrying to, nor turning from, the goal;**
**Not mourning for the things that disappear**
**In the dim past, nor holding back in fear**
**From what the future veils; but with a whole**
**And happy heart, that pays its toll**
**To Youth and Age, and travels on with cheer.**

*—Henry Van Dyke*

**To keep the heart unwrinkled,
to be hopeful, kindly, cheerful, reverent—
that is to triumph over old age.**

*—Thomas B. Aldrich*

**Now the God of hope fill you with
all joy and peace in believing,
that ye may abound in hope, through
the power of the Holy Ghost.**

*—Romans 15:13*

Lord, help me remember that you are the God of hope. You don't want me to feel sad or hopeless. It isn't your plan for me to live in fear or doubt. Help me to feel and access the power of the Holy Spirit. I know that through your Spirit I will find the hope, joy, and peace you have promised to your people.

**He will swallow up death in victory; and the Lord God will wipe away tears from off all faces; and the rebuke of his people shall he take away from off all the earth: for the Lord hath spoken it.**

*—Isaiah 25:8*

Lord, it hurts to see those we love with tears in their eyes. We want so desperately to take away their pain and comfort them. But as we go to their sides in their time of need, we should not go alone. Only you can offer true comfort. Please add your comfort to ours as we support our friends through these trying times.

**Comfort isn't ours alone—it is to be shared with those we encounter each day.**

Hope is a verb, an action, a doing. Hope is a force that keeps us from giving up, even when it might look wiser to do so. Always have hope that things will get better. Hope is our lifeline to a God who will never abandon us. Hope is the anchor that keeps us connected to his will, his love, and his strength. Always have hope.

How grateful we are, God of knowledge, that you created us so curious. In your wisdom, it is the searcher turning over every leaf who finds four-leaf clovers; the doubter who invents; and the determined, like a duckling pecking its way from the shell, who emerges strong enough to fly.

When your dreams seem unreachable, trust that the future will lighten your burdens, smooth your path, and urge you on to a brighter tomorrow.

**Hope is a waking dream.**

*—Aristotle*

**Therefore we are buried with him by baptism into death: that like as Christ was raised up from the dead by the glory of the Father, even so we also should walk in newness of life.**

*—Romans 6:4*

Lord, today my heart goes out to all those whose past mistakes weigh them down and make any vision they have of their future dreary at best. Oh, that they might know you and the saving grace you bring! Draw near to them today, Lord. Reveal yourself to them in a way that will reach them, and through your mercy and forgiveness, bestow upon them a new vision—a new hope.

**I stood up straight and worked**
**My veritable work. And as the soul**
**Which grows within a child**
**makes the child grow,**
**Or, as the fiery sap, the touch of God,**
**Careering through a tree, dilates the bark**
**And toughs with scale and knob,**
**before it strikes**
**The summer foliage out in a green flame—**
**So life, in deepening with me, deepened all**
**The course I took, the work I did.**

*—Elizabeth Barrett Browning*

**That by two immutable things, in which it was impossible for God to lie, we might have a strong consolation, who have fled for refuge to lay hold upon the hope set before us: Which hope we have as an anchor of the soul, both sure and stedfast, and which entereth into that within the veil.**

*—Hebrews 6:18–19*

Hope is an anchor to the soul. It can keep us from drifting aimlessly, getting caught in whirlpools, or running into sandbars. This anchor is essential in a world so full of various waves. Sometimes those waves slap us from behind; sometimes we see them coming but cannot get out of the way. In all cases, hope ties us to safety. The waves come and go in their fury or playfulness—but hope is always there.

**The next day John seeth Jesus coming unto him, and saith, Behold the Lamb of God, which taketh away the sin of the world.**

*—John 1:29*

Lord, the world just wasn't ready for your appearance by the Jordan. There you were, the King they so desired; yet most didn't know you. Let us welcome you into our world today as wholeheartedly as John the Baptist did when you appeared in the flesh! For you came to be our hope and our salvation.

**The greatest burden that we have to carry in life is self. The most difficult thing we have to manage is self. . . . In laying off your burdens therefore, the first one you must get rid of is yourself. You must hand yourself and all your inward experiences, your temptations, your temperament, your . . . feelings all over into the care and keeping of our God. And leave them there. He made you, He understands you, He knows how to manage you, and you must trust Him to do it.**

*—Hannah Whitall Smith*

**Behold, I will bring it health and cure, and I will cure them, and will reveal unto them the abundance of peace and truth.**

*—Jeremiah 33:6*

Bring your cool caress to the foreheads of those suffering fever. By your spirit, lift the spirits of the bedridden and give comfort to those in pain. Strengthen all entrusted with the care of the infirm today, and give them renewed energy for their tasks. Fill them with hope. And remind us all that heaven awaits—where we will all be whole and healthy before you, brothers and sisters forever.

God, sometimes I wish I could be saved from the struggle and pain of learning the hard way. But that's not your plan, and I need to be willing to wait patiently as you work gently from the inside out. Please grant me some strength in this time of uncertainty.

**Hope and patience are two sovereign remedies for all, the surest reposals, the softest cushions to lean on in adversity.**

*—Robert Burton*

God, we know that pain has produced some wisdom in our lives, but it has also created cynicism and fear. People turn on us, reject us, hurt us, and none of us wants to play the fool more than once, so we're tempted to close off our hearts to people and to you. But relationships that bring meaning and joy require vulnerability. Help us trust you to be our truest friend and to lead us to the kind of community that will bring healing and hope rather than destruction.

**I'd like to pray to be spared of all pain, but life is full of pain. No one escapes it. Better to ask God to be near whenever it comes.**

**O welcome pure-ey'd Faith,**
**white-handed Hope,**
**Thou hovering angel girt with**
**golden wings...**
**I see you visibly and now believe**
**That he, the Supreme good...**
**Would send a glistening Guardian**
**if need were**
**To keep my life and honor unassailed.**

*—John Milton*

**The people that walked in darkness have seen a great light: they that dwell in the land of the shadow of death, upon them hath the light shined.**

*—Isaiah 9:2*

The prophet Isaiah wrote a number of inspired words from God that pointed to the coming of Christ to Earth. In this passage, he speaks of a great light shining on those living in a dark land. Spiritual darkness is the deepest kind of darkness. One may live in the darkness of being physically blind and yet have the light of Christ, which brings meaning, joy, and hope. Without the light of Christ in a life, there is something missing in the soul.

**Whatsoever thy hand findeth to do, do it with thy might; for there is no work, nor device, nor knowledge, nor wisdom, in the grave, whither thou goest.**

—*Ecclesiastes 9:10*

Today I am tired, Lord. There seem to be too many things on my to-do list and too few hours in the day. And still, I know what a blessing it is to have work to do and to live a purpose-filled life. Thank you for tasks large and small that give meaning to our days, Lord. May we always do each one as if we were doing it only for you. And may we never assume we can do anything without your direction and energy.

**Remembering without ceasing your work of faith, and labour of love, and patience of hope in our Lord Jesus Christ, in the sight of God and our Father.**

*—1 Thessalonians 1:3*

Hope says, "No matter how many times I fall, I will stand and start again." For a person of hope is not one who never falls, but one who picks herself up one more time than she falls.

**Hardship helps a woman recognize good fortune.**

**Till he fill thy mouth with laughing, and thy lips with rejoicing.**

*—Job 8:21*

There is a choice, O God, when I spot the crayon markings on the wall, the spilled food, the wet towel on the bed. I have equal breath to scream or laugh. I feel the insistent tickle of my funny bone, and I know which choice you will. Join us as we laugh our way into a better mood.

**Let thy mercy, O Lord, be upon us, according as we hope in thee.**

*—Psalm 33:22*

Like the evergreen, hope never dies, but stands tall and mighty against the coldest winter winds until the summer sun returns to warm its outstretched branches.

In a silent world, no voice is heard,
No bark of a dog or song of a bird,
No strains of music or chime of a bell;
A noiseless, mysterious place to dwell.

But there is hope in this daunting place,
And happiness comes to a deaf child's face,
When, with his hands,
His thoughts he can share,
He has learned to sign,
Because you are there.

You lift a cloud from the youngster's heart,
And she can smile because
You did your part.
You've lightened the load she has to bear.
It isn't as hard, because you are there.

Your smiling face greets them each day.
Your simple gestures chase their fears away.
The love that you give shows them you care.
Their world is better, because you are there.

**Being confident of this very thing, that he which hath begun a good work in you will perform it until the day of Jesus Christ.**

*—Philippians 1:6*

O Lord, what a comfort it is to know that you are working to perfect us even on days when we feel anything but perfect. One day all creation will be perfected. How we look forward to that day when our faith is fully realized, and we are complete in you!

**Trust in the Lord with all thine heart; and lean not unto thine own understanding.**

*—Proverbs 3:5*

Sometimes I work so hard to control everything that I need to be reminded to take faith and "let go." Last night my head was in a whirl: I lay in bed and stared into the darkness, worrying about bills, my workload, if my son would ever get off the bench on his football team, if my husband and I would have time to care for the yard before the frost. My mind churned as I envisioned schemes, schedules, emails I might write, ways to exert control. It was only when I "let go" and decided to give my concerns over to you that I earned some measure of peace, and was able to sleep. Lord, thank you for your support and guidance as I navigate my busy days. May I have the faith to trust you over my own understanding.

**Child, even this day, trust!**
**And to-morrow have faith,**
**And on all to-morrows!**
**The darkness grow less.**
**Trust! And each day when first**
**gleams the dawn-breath,**
**Awake thou to pray;**
**God is wakeful to bless!**

*—Victor Hugo, "Trust in God"*

**Brethren, I count not myself to have apprehended: but this one thing I do, forgetting those things which are behind, and reaching forth unto those things which are before, I press toward the mark for the prize of the high calling of God in Christ Jesus.**

*—Philippians 3:13–14*

Lord, what good does it do to dwell on past mistakes? You tell us to look forward with hope, not backward, and yet we play failures and sins over and over in our minds. We know those thoughts aren't from you, Lord. Keep our minds focused on the truth of your salvation and on the new life we have in you.

**In thee, O Lord, do I put my trust:
let me never be put to confusion.**

*—Psalm 71:1*

Help me grieve and go on, Lord Jesus, go on in new ways you will reveal to me, as I make my faltering way as far as I can. Hold me while I name and mourn all I have lost, weeping and wailing like the abandoned child I feel I am. Then, in time and with you to lean on, I can focus on what I have left.

**God does not leave you comfortless.
He provides you a shoulder to lean on
and soothing words of friends
to ease your sorrow.**

**That being justified by his grace, we should be made heirs according to the hope of eternal life.**

*—Titus 3:7*

**Hope springs eternal in the human breast:**
**Man never is, but always to be, blest.**
**The soul, uneasy and confin'd from home**
**Rests and expatiates in a life to come.**

*—Alexander Pope*

Lord, you are here,
Lord, you are there.
You are wherever we go.
Lord, you guide us,
Lord, you protect us.
You are wherever we go.
Lord, we need you,
Lord, we trust you,
You are wherever we go.
Lord, we love you,

Lord, we praise you,
You are wherever we go.

**And Mizpah; for he said,**
**The Lord watch between me and thee,**
**when we are absent one from another.**

—*Genesis 31:49*

O Lord, how hard it is to say goodbye to loved ones visiting from thousands of miles away. Help us be mindful that even on days when we can't see their smiles or feel their hugs, you are lovingly watching over all of us. We are connected in a special way through you, Lord. Spiritually, we are never far apart.

**Therefore with joy shall ye draw water out of the wells of salvation.**

*—Isaiah 12:3*

When grief fills my heart, Father, whether I'm feeling loss, shame, betrayal, or some other sorrow, I know it's temporary, even though at times it feels as though it will never go away. I know that your future for me is hope and joy, and when it comes, I will not reject it. Strengthen me with your joy today, Father. I need it to lift up my soul.

What a beautiful and precious dichotomy hope is. Delicate as a flower, yet as strong as steel, hope refuses to surrender, even in the face of great adversity. Both fragile as a finely sculpted glass figurine, and as fierce as a courageous lion, hope stands up to the greatest

challenges. Hope promises the warmth of a sun-drenched day, and the resplendent starlit night.

**Enjoy all of creation, each leaf and flower and every small pebble along the way. Embrace the hope of each new morning, and the last ray of sunshine to fall at day's end.**

God, thank you for sometimes reminding me that in the center of chaos lies the seed of new opportunity and that things are not always as awful as they seem at first. I often forget that what starts out bad can end up great and that it is all a matter of my own perspective. Amen.

**But to do good and to communicate forget not: for with such sacrifices God is well pleased.**

*—Hebrews 13:16*

Whatever tests in life you're facing, whether it's a challenge of relationships, finances, or your career, the loving Spirit that created you is always available to guide you into a better life.

I awoke at dawn one morning
From a restless night of sorrow,
Praying that with the daylight
Might come a bright tomorrow.
My heart as cold and hopeless
As winter's deepest chill,
I cried out for understanding
And to know my Father's will.
While treading up a garden path
Hushed in the fragrant air;
I spied a tender rose,
Its petals bowed as if in prayer.
As I gazed in silent awe,
It occurred to me—He knows!
The tears my Lord has shed for me
Are the dew upon the rose.

**The Lord also shall roar out of Zion, and utter his voice from Jerusalem; and the heavens and the earth shall shake: but the Lord will be the hope of his people, and the strength of the children of Israel.**

*—Joel 3:16*

Living in difficult times requires us to maintain a positive, hopeful attitude about the future. Having hope is vital for our mental, physical, and spiritual health.

Lord, help me move into the future with a steadfast spirit, looking forward in faith and hope and trusting in the promises you have made to your people.

Today I make a covenant to you that I will choose hope. If I encounter disappointment, I will choose hope. If confronted with temptation, I will choose hope. In the face of fear, I will choose hope. If I sense doubt washing over me, I will choose hope. If I feel angry, I will choose hope. Instead of giving in to sadness or despair, I will choose hope.

In all things that come my way today, Lord, I am determined to choose hope. Regardless of what happened in the past, today—through you—I am strong enough to choose hope.

Sometimes it feels as though our journey is mapped out. As children we are scheduled, shuttled, and herded. Adult life falls into a routine we can both rely on and resent. But every day there is an open road before us, a path of our choosing marked only by God's love.

**God's plans, like lilies,**
**pure and white, unfold;**
**We must not tear the**
**close-shut leaves apart;**
**Time will reveal the chalices of gold.**

*—Mary Louise Riley Smith*

Lord of hope, I am touched by all the things that happen because of one word or one act. Something that seems insignificant can make a huge difference. One visit to a worship service can start a person on the journey of faith. One teacher can make the difference for a student. One mountain-top experience or religious revival can call a person to a new vocation. One senseless tragedy can spur a community to open a teen center. One candle lit in the darkness can chase away the dark.

Not wasting a moment, a child leaps from sleep and skips into a wonder-filled day, assuming it to be one! See, too, how they jump to their feet after a fall or rise in curiosity after disappointment, knowing more good than bad sums up each day. Ah, an example to follow.

**Be ye mindful always of his covenant; the word which he commanded to a thousand generations.**

*—1 Chronicles 16:15*

Almighty God, our faith in you is undergirded by your faithfulness. No matter how many times we turn away, you patiently wait for us to return to you. Instill in us that same sense of honor and faithfulness that is yours, Lord. May we be as faithful to you as you have been to us.

The dawn of a new day brings new possibilities and challenges. We hope they'll all be good ones, but we know they won't, and that's where God comes in. Lord, thank you for being a God of new beginnings.

Even in my toughest moments, Lord, I yearn to grow into fullest flower. Give me a faith as resilient and determined as dandelions pushing up through cracks in the pavement.

God promises us his comfort, but he also uses us as his agents to comfort others. In fact, the difficulties we've gone through often give us the ability to reassure others who are now going through the same experiences. How will God use you to extend comfort to someone else?

**God does not comfort us to make us comfortable, but to make us comforters.**

*—John Henry Jowett*

Lord, give me the faith to take the next step, even when I don't know what lies head. Give me the assurance that even if I stumble and fall, you'll pick me up and put me back on the path. And give me the confidence that, even if I lose hope, you will never lose me.

**My help cometh from the Lord, which made heaven and earth.**

*—Psalm 121:2*

Lord, today I will be in the spotlight. I've been given an opportunity to be in front of a group, and I want to do a good job conveying my important message. Be with me, Lord; I know that I can accomplish very little without your help, but anything is possible with your guidance. Keep me focused not on myself, but on the insight I have to share.

We know you, Lord, in the changing seasons: in leaves blazing gently in fall beauty; in winter's snow sculptures. We know you in arid desert cactus bloom and in migration of whale and spawn of fish and turtle. In the blending of the seasons, we feel your renewing, steadfast care, and worries lose their power to overwhelm. The list of your hope-filled marvels is endless.

**They that fear thee will be glad when they see me; because I have hoped in thy word.**

*—Psalm 119:74*

Lord, I do believe! And because of my hope of life with you in eternity, there is all the more meaning for life today. There's meaning in my choices, my relationships, my work, my play, my worship. It all matters, it all counts, and I live knowing one day I'll stand in your presence with great joy.

**I wait for the Lord, my soul doth wait, and in his word do I hope. My soul waiteth for the Lord more than they that watch for the morning: I say, more than they that watch for the morning. Let Israel hope in the Lord: for with the Lord there is mercy, and with him is plenteous redemption.**

*—Psalm 130:5–7*

**Take my yoke upon you, and learn of me; for I am meek and lowly in heart: and ye shall find rest unto your souls.**

*—Matthew 11:29*

Lord, if ever there was a day when I needed your rest, it is today. Nothing seems to be going right, and just carrying around my to-do list is exhausting—it is so long! Please help me sort out which things really need to be done and which I can let go.

**A wise woman trades her to-do list for the Lord's.**

**Jesus beheld them, and said unto them, With men this is impossible; but with God all things are possible.**

*—Matthew 19:26*

From my perspective, a lot of things look tough. I have the responsibility of maintaining a long-term commitment to my husband and children, even on days when they aren't exactly endearing. There is the responsibility of dealing fairly and kindly with my coworkers, even when my boss is being a jerk and my peers are self-absorbed and mean-spirited. And then there is God's expectation that I will put him first in my life. There are days when juggling these responsibilities seems practically impossible. But Jesus said we don't have to do everything by ourselves; in fact, with God's help we can do the inconceivable. For "With God all things are possible," Jesus said.

**Dear God, help me to trust you for the impossible. Thank you for giving me the confidence and courage to deal with difficult challenges. With you, nothing is impossible.**

**For I know the thoughts that I think toward you, saith the Lord, thoughts of peace, and not of evil, to give you an expected end.**

*—Jeremiah 29:11*

God has plans to give us a future with hope and peace. God often works in unassuming human deeds. Our sense of hope in the future may not come with lightning bolts or grand plans. It may be as simple as an unexpected call from a friend after we received bad news from a doctor; an offer of help in organizing a letter-writing campaign; a parent who holds on to the bike again and again until the child masters the two-wheeler. It may be a word or a hug, a letter or a community protest—but we see the possibilities in the future, and we are filled with hope.

God, thank you for giving me a sense of hope about the future.

**In hope that sends a shining ray**
**far down the future's broad'ning way,**
**in peace that only thou canst give,**
**with thee, O Master, let me live.**

*—Washington Gladden, "O Master, Let Me Walk With Thee"*

**Ye have wept in the ears of the Lord.**

*—Numbers 11:18*

Mothers hear the phrase "it's not fair!" regularly, Lord. Are we really being unfair in our dealings with our children, or are they merely complaining?

Just as the Israelites complained to you while being fed in the wilderness, so today's children feel cheated because a gift is the "wrong" shape, brand, or color.

Lord of peace, wrap us in your love, and dispel the cloud of discontent that hangs over our children. Guard us from weeping in your ear. Take away our complaining spirits, and sprinkle us with the gentle rain of forgiveness.

Lord, I pray to you tonight for strength. I am going through a tough time, and I have faith that you will see me through. But until then, I ask that you give me the extra energy, resilience, and courage needed to do your will and not make more bad choices or mistakes. I know a bright solution is on the horizon. You have never let me down before. I ask that you keep me in your comforting presence until I stand in the light again. Amen.

**Be ye therefore followers of God, as dear children; And walk in love, as Christ also hath loved us, and hath given himself for us an offering and a sacrifice to God for a sweetsmelling savour.**

*—Ephesians 5:1–2*

Lord, from this past year I'd like to save in the scrapbook of my life just those days that brought you glory—days when in spite of my self-absorption and often worldly focus, you were able to accomplish something through me. Those are the days I cherish, Lord. Help me to move into the next year more available—more open—to living such scrapbook-worthy days.

**That they might set their hope in God,**
**and not forget the works of God,**
**but keep his commandments.**

*—Psalm 78:7*

Hope is one of God's great works. It comes as a gift, not something that we have to earn. It comes through the actions of others, but it also comes more mysteriously as a whisper in the night, a dawning clarity of direction, or a sudden burst of confidence. God gives hope to people in all times and places, in all situations and circumstances.

God, hear my prayer. Bless me with patience and a steadfast heart to help me get through such emotionally trying times. Heal the wounds of my heart and soul with the soothing balm of your comforting presence, so that I may be able to love and to live again. Amen.

**Hope keeps the heart whole.**

*—Antony Brewert*

Lord, motherhood is full of trials that have tested my faith. And, yes, I have developed perseverance and maturity. In the midst of these trials, I am often ready to give up, to weep and wail over my misfortune; but you are there, Lord, to comfort me. You come to me with your hope and healing touch to wipe away my sorrow. With your help, Father, I have so far managed to survive each trial intact, with the joy far outweighing the pain. As I hug each of my children and hold them tight, I thank you, Lord.

# A Prayer by Paul

**For this cause I bow my knees unto the Father of our Lord Jesus Christ, Of whom the whole family in heaven and earth is named, That he would grant you, according to the riches of his glory, to be strengthened with might by his Spirit in the inner man; That Christ may dwell in your hearts by faith; that ye, being rooted and grounded in love, May be able to comprehend with all saints what is the breadth, and length, and depth, and height; And to know the love of Christ, which passeth knowledge, that ye might be filled with all the fulness of God. Now unto him that is able to do exceeding abundantly above all that we ask or think, according to the power that worketh in us, Unto him be glory in the church by Christ Jesus throughout all ages, world without end. Amen.**

*—Ephesians 3:14–21*

Two ears, one mouth? Perhaps a hint, subtle or not, about what is more important in life, Great God. Make me at least as ready to listen as I am to talk. Give me patience to listen to the concerns, the hopes, and the dreams of these important people called family, for that is how we connect. There are times to talk and times to listen. Please help me to know the difference.

**If we were supposed to talk more than we listen, we would have two mouths and one ear.**

*—Mark Twain*

Heavenly Father, you are the God of hope. You are a God who sends rainbows after rain, makes joy out of sorrow, and turns Good Friday deaths into Easter resurrections. Thank you for hope.

**Through faith we understand that the worlds were framed by the word of God, so that things which are seen were not made of things which do appear.**

*—Hebrews 11:3*

Father, your Word makes it clear to me that the life of faith is not passive. While we wait for you to answer prayer, grant wisdom, and open doors, we also keep our minds sharp and our hearts strengthened by reading and studying your Word, by meeting with you in prayer, and by finding

encouragement among other believers. These are the disciplines our souls need to stay focused on ever-present hope.

**But they that wait upon the Lord shall renew their strength; they shall mount up with wings as eagles; they shall run, and not be weary; and they shall walk, and not faint.**

*—Isaiah 40:31*

To be strong may not be a matter of physical strength but rather an orientation toward God, who gives us incredible courage in the face of a world that is often filled with fear and violence. To be strong is to know that Jesus is calling, that God is coming, that hope rests in God.

I begin my mornings with a time of prayer and meditation, a time of waiting on the Lord. I pray for God's presence, asking for courage, and because God promises to be with me in all circumstances, I have hope. I can go through each day hopeful and with confidence that God will guide me, help me, support me, and challenge me.

**Now the Lord of peace himself give you peace always by all means. The Lord be with you all.**

*—2 Thessalonians 3:16*

Lord, you who brought peace in the midst of the storm are the only one who can bring peace to our world today. How much anger we see raging around us, Lord. And the conflicts are not limited to wars on foreign soil. Rather they rage in the hearts and minds of many of us. Be the source of peace in every gathering storm, Lord.

You are the Prince of Peace, and we need you desperately.

Lord, I gladly put my hope in you. You are all the things your Word says you are: my strength, my shield, and my salvation. In a world filled with darkness and doubt, I expect you to refresh me with your light and give me joy.

**Who bids me hope, and**
**in that charming word**
**Has peace and transport**
**to my soul restor'd.**

*—George Lyttleton*

**For his anger endureth but a moment; in his favour is life: weeping may endure for a night, but joy cometh in the morning.**

*—Psalm 30:5*

Lord, only you can comfort us when we grieve. The heaviness we feel at such times can make even breathing a struggle. But you, O Lord, stay close. You fill us with your peace and your comfort. You never let us retreat completely from your light into the darkness of despair. And finally, in your time, you restore joy to our souls. We are ever so grateful, O Great Comforter.

Dear God, please send your peace to calm us when we're overwhelmed. Your presence wipes away depression and despair. It renews our hope and lifts our hearts. Amen.

**Faith makes all evil good to us, and all good better; unbelief makes all good evil, and all evil worse. Faith laughs at the shaking of the spear; unbelief trembles at the shaking of a leaf, unbelief starves the soul; faith finds food in famine, and a table in the wilderness. In the greatest danger, faith said, "I have a great God." When outward strength is broken, faith rests on the promises. In the midst of sorrow, faith draws the string out of every trouble, and takes out the bitterness from every affliction.**

*—Robert Cecil*

Creator, help me to remember who I am. Before I became a friend, there was me. Before I became a wife, there was me. Before I became a mother, there was me. Guide me back to that person that I gave away so long ago. Give me back to "me," and restore my wholeness, so that I can then become a better friend, a better wife, and a better mother. Direct me back onto the path you set out for me so long ago, before I got sidetracked by the roles and duties of life. Help me, Divine One; help me find my way back home again.

**But he knoweth the way that I take: when he hath tried me, I shall come forth as gold.**

*—Job 23:10*

I think it's good for me to be able to see my frustrations, difficulties, and sorrows as "proving grounds" for my growing trust in you, Lord. From difficulty finding fulfilling work to bills I'm struggling to pay to a disagreement with my husband, life brings every kind of opportunity for me to look to you for help. Today is a great day to choose to not get wrapped around my own axle when I'm faced with frustrations and fears. I'm putting all of the "proving ground" stuff I'm facing right now into your hands, and I trust you with the outcome.

**Rejoicing in hope; patient in tribulation; continuing instant in prayer.**

*—Romans 12:12*

We see every day the benefits of a "coffee break,": at our jobs, from our routines, to catch up with loved ones. But we must also take time to nurture our faith in our daily lives in addition to times of need. To check in with our faith every day, as though it were an old friend, reminds us that God's work is everything.

Lord, we understand that there are and will always be problems in our lives, but please remind us of your presence when the problems seem insurmountable. We want to believe that you know best. We hope to remain patient as we search for purpose. Amen.

**Patience and persistence are companions of hope.**

**And the Lord shall guide thee continually, and satisfy thy soul in drought, and make fat thy bones: and thou shalt be like a watered garden, and like a spring of water, whose waters fail not.**

*—Isaiah 58:11*

Lord, the older I get, the more challenging I find it to make big changes in my life. Transitions can be great stressors, but I know they can also turn into wonderful opportunities. Help me have eyes of hope and a heart of anticipation so that I can turn my face toward the changes you bring and smile at them, even as I may be grieving the loss of some of the old things. Remind me that you are already there in the changes, that you have ample grace and comfort for me along the way as I learn to trust you in my new circumstances.

Lord, I'm looking forward to this new phase of my life. It is full of promise and hope, though I know that challenges will surely come as well. I know you have all the courage, strength, faithfulness, and love I need to meet each moment from a perspective of peace. I just need to stay tethered to you in prayer, listening for your

Spirit to guide me and turn my thoughts continually back toward you. That's the key to a good life.

It takes faith to go beyond what others know—to explore new ideas, to stand on our convictions that there is something more, and to trust that God has called us to discover it.

**If you do not hope, you will not find what is beyond your hopes.**

*—St. Clement of Alexandria*

The scriptures are for our encouragement. The notion that the Bible is no longer relevant to our modern way of life is a mistaken notion: "For whatsoever things were written aforetime were written for our learning, that we through patience and comfort of the scriptures might have hope" (Romans 15:4). People's essential needs, drives, and desires have not changed, and the Bible's contents address the human condition as no other writings on Earth. From the account of Creation to the story of redemption, the pages of scripture speak eternal encouragement and hope to our hearts.

**Now faith is the substance of things hoped for, the evidence of things not seen.**

*—Hebrews 11:1*

Faith is knowing without seeing, believing without fully understanding, trusting without touching God who is ever faithful.

**What can be hoped for which is not believed?**

*—Augustine of Hippo*

**The God of my rock; in him will I trust: he is my shield, and the horn of my salvation, my high tower, and my refuge, my saviour; thou savest me from violence.**

*—2 Samuel 22:3*

God, it's so hard to see your will in suffering. But while I can't understand your ways, I trust your heart. And so I cling to the faith that has sustained me through so many heartaches before, knowing that although it may be all I have, it's also all I need. Amen.

Rejoice when I run into problems?
Know trials are good for me?
Things like that aren't easy—
Learning to live patiently.

Growing in grace is a process.
Developing character hurts.
Becoming more Christ-like in all things
Is an everyday process called work.

But if I have faith it is possible.
Faith knowing God loves and cares—
That all my burdens and trials
He also feels and shares.

**The Lord is good, a strong hold in the day of trouble; and he knoweth them that trust in him.**

*—Nahum 1:7*

Lord, I know that if life were smooth sailing, there would be no need for faith. I thank you for the opportunity to trust you tenaciously, in spite of the obstacles in my path. Give me a fresh start today, Lord. I trust you to see me through any trouble I encounter today.

To live in hope means to expect our longings will be fulfilled. When we hold that image of fulfillment constantly, we cannot help but notice all the ways in which our lives are blessed.

**Love children especially,**
**for like the angels they too are sinless,**
**and they live to soften and purify**
**our hearts, and as it were, to guide us.**

*—Fyodor Dostoevsky*

**Nay, in all these things we are more than conquerors through him that loved us.**

*—Romans 8:37*

Lord, today I pray for all those who are suffering from any sort of addiction. Whether it's drugs, gambling, overeating, or compulsive exercising, Lord, addiction keeps them from being the people you designed them to be. Their obsession separates them from you and walls them off from their loved ones as well. Break through and release them from their chains, Lord. Give them the strength to put their troubles behind them and find hope in a new life with you.

**Teach me to feel another's woe,**
**To hide the fault I see;**
**That mercy I to others show,**
**That mercy show to me.**

*—Alexander Pope*

May I have a moment to talk with you, O God? I know there is so much going on in the world that requires your attention. It's just that sometimes I feel tension getting a grip on me and worry clouds my view. This distances me from you and from everything in my life. I pray for the freedom to worry less. I want to simply trust you more.

**Cast away your anxieties and place your trust in the Lord.**

**I can do all things through Christ which strengtheneth me.**

*—Philippians 4:13*

Lord, I am overwhelmed with the whirl of activity around me. Getting ready for work, making meals, doing dishes, giving rides, running errands, fielding phone calls, keeping appointments, dealing with calamities. . . how do I fit it all in? I am crumbling under the weight of each day, only to find that I need to wake up and do it all over again the next day.

**Hope thou in God: for I shall yet praise him, who is the health of my countenance, and my God.**

*—Psalm 42:11*

As we learn to put our hope and trust you, God, we discover your strengthening presence in various places and people. Wherever we encounter shelter, comfort, rest, and peace, we are bound to hear your voice, welcoming us. And in whomever we find hope, truth, love, gentleness, and humility, we are sure to hear your heartbeat, assuring us that you will always be near. Thank you, God. Amen.

**Hope deferred maketh the heart sick: but when the desire cometh, it is a tree of life.**

*—Proverbs 13:12*

We all know the sting of being heartsick. Loss, unrequited love, unfulfilled expectations—any of these can lead to the feeling of our heart being sick. The passage above tells us that it is actually putting off hope that truly makes our hearts sick. God knows the pain we experience in this life. He knows how to comfort us. If we cling to hope and turn to God, despite all that life may throw at us, we are sure to find ourselves filled with peace and joy.

**The root of faith produces the flower of heart-joy. We may not at the first rejoice, but it comes in due time. We trust the Lord when we are sad, and in due season He so answers our confidence that our faith turns to fruition and we rejoice in the Lord. Doubt breeds distress, but trust means joy in the long run.**

*—Charles Spurgeon*

**I will greatly rejoice in the Lord, my soul shall be joyful in my God; for he hath clothed me with the garments of salvation, he hath covered me with the robe of righteousness, as a bridegroom decketh himself with ornaments, and as a bride adorneth herself with her jewels.**

*—Isaiah 61:10*

These are fantastic word pictures! Salvation worn like a garment,

righteousness donned like a robe, and belonging to you revealed as a bride's glittering accessories—that's how you describe my life in you. And yet, I don't quite see it that way right now. Please give me hope to believe this reality.

Father God, teach me to trust your protection. It's so hard sometimes to find my way home. The nights get dark. The clouds hide the stars. If I could learn to hold the hand of your angels, I know you would lead me all the way.

**Like the lighthouse beacon, faith guides our way through the fog of fear, doubt, and uncertainty to the sea of clarity beyond.**

**The Lord is nigh unto all them that call upon him, to all that call upon him in truth.**

*—Psalm 145:18*

Lord, I thank you for your faithfulness. Your promise to be near me and to hear my prayers gives me comfort and hope. I need your continual guidance. No matter how hopeless a situation may seem, I know you have the answers I need. As I pray, I feel your peace filling up my parched spirit and bringing sweet relief. I feel your wisdom directing my thoughts toward new ideas and solutions. Forgive me, Lord, for the times I have prayed selfishly or have failed to pray at all.

**In returning and rest shall ye be saved; in quietness and in confidence shall be your strength.**

*—Isaiah 30:15*

Tossing leaves onto a fire, we name them as regrets and failures from which we choose to be free. We trust you to redeem even these, our deadest moments. They, like autumn leaves, can make the brightest blaze.

Stir new possibilities into life from the embers; fan the sparks of dreams so that we may become one with your purpose for us. It is the root from which we, leaf and human life, begin and from which the most amazing new creation can burst into being, a flame in the darkness.

Dear Father, we wonder why the pleasures of the past have left us. It is difficult to realize that they will be replaced by other pleasures. Please help us to place our trust and hope in you as you reconstruct our lives. Amen.

**Trust the past to God's mercy, the present to God's love, and the future to God's providence.**

*—Augustine of Hippo*

**And the very God of peace sanctify you wholly; and I pray God your whole spirit and soul and body be preserved blameless unto the coming of our Lord Jesus Christ. Faithful is he that calleth you, who also will do it.**

*—1 Thessalonians 5:23–24*

Maybe it's bitterness. Maybe it's timidity. Maybe it's pride. Or maybe we tend to gossip or complain. Whatever sins we struggle with, though, we should never lose heart! Often it's our weaknesses that keep us close to God. When we find ourselves overwhelmed with feelings of bitterness, it's a signal that we're not devoting enough time to prayer and reflection. God is faithful, and it's only through him that we can overcome our weaknesses. So rather than becoming discouraged that we still have the same old struggles, we need to look at our struggles as strings binding us to our heavenly Father.

**It is better to trust in the Lord than to put confidence in princes.**

*—Psalm 118:9*

Our fellow human beings will let us down. They will disappoint us, not come through for us, and even, at times, hurt us. This is because they are human. They may love us, but they won't always be there for us. Only God will be consistent and true when we put our hope and trust in him. There is one who never abandons us: God.

Friends and loved ones are the walls that we build our homes with, but God alone is the foundation. Strong, unmovable, and steadfast, God is the basis upon which we build all of our relationships, goals, and dreams. There can be no walls, doors, or windows without first having a solid foundation. Though we have human and animal companions that care for us, we put our faith first in our creator, our Father, our God.

Heavenly Father, in you I place my faith. In you I cast my cares. In you I rest in hope. In you I find my peace. Amen.

**Hope is the parent of faith.**

—*Cyrus Augustus Bartol*

**Be merciful unto me, O God, be merciful unto me: for my soul trusteth in thee: yea, in the shadow of thy wings will I make my refuge, until these calamities be overpast.**

*—Psalm 57:1*

**Lord, help me trust you enough to tear down the walls of fear and doubt.**

**Ah! What would the world be to us**
**If the children were no more?**
**We should dread the desert behind us**
**Worse than the dark before.**

*—Henry Wadsworth Longfellow*

You have made things problematic again, Lord, and I need to see that all this upheaval can be a good thing. Help me, Lord. And thank you for showing me that a thoroughly comfortable existence can rob me of real life.

**For thus saith the high and lofty One that inhabiteth eternity, whose name is Holy; I dwell in the high and holy place, with him also that is of a contrite and humble spirit, to revive the spirit of the humble, and to revive the heart of the contrite ones.**

*—Isaiah* 57:15

Lord, in my darkest moments, it is easy to despair and fear that you have given up on me. It would be understandable for you to be angry and disappointed and leave me to my ruin. How comforting it is to know that the minute I regret what I have done and turn to you, you are right where you have been all along—by my side, ready to embrace and carry me until I am strong enough to take a step on my own. Thank you for your faithfulness, Lord—especially when I least deserve it.

In this time of great change, help me, God of tomorrow, tomorrow, and tomorrow, to trust your guiding presence. You will light my path. That's all I really need.

**Hope is faith holding out its hand in the dark.**

*—George Iles*

**Faith lifts the staggering soul on one side, Hope supports it on the other. Experience says it must be, and Love says—let it be.**

*—Elizabeth Ann Seton*

**Yea, though I walk through the valley of the shadow of death, I will fear no evil: for thou art with me; thy rod and thy staff they comfort me.**

*—Psalm 23:4*

Within the valleys of mountainous terrain, darkness lingers long in the morning and swoops down to settle swiftly in the evening. The taller the surrounding mountaintops, the deeper and darker the valley. The psalmist has one of these deep valleys in mind—a place where the path is shadowy and a chill is always in the air.

Yet here, in what some might call a godforsaken place, the psalmist surprises us with these words: "I will fear no evil: for thou art with me." He surprises and comforts us with his reminder that when we follow the Lord our shepherd, there is no such thing as a godforsaken place.

**For in thee, O Lord, do I hope:
thou wilt hear, O Lord my God.**

*—Psalm 38:15*

Lord, give us hope. Please help us to put our trust in you. Amen.

**Hope blooms like a beautiful rose amidst the thorns of life.**

**But when the fullness of the time was come, God sent forth his Son, made of a woman, made under the law, To redeem them that were under the law, that we might receive the adoption of sons.**

*—Galatians 4:4–5*

Father, it's as if time itself was aware of your plan to redeem humanity through your son. In this verse I'm reminded of your perfect timing—that nothing you do is by accident or happenstance. Jesus came at precisely the right time in history to carry out your wonderful purposes. I'll trust you, then, with the timing in my life. I'll stop fretting and wait patiently. You are in control, and I know you have a plan.

Hope is the aspiration of the soul, the persistence of the mind, and the affirmation of the heart.

**Hope is the most pleasing Passion of the Soul.**

*—Eliza Haywood*

When my way is drear,
Precious Lord, linger near.
When the day is almost gone,
Hear my cry, hear my call,
Hold my hand, lest I fall,
Precious Lord, take my hand,
lead me home.

God's Word brings hope. The movie title *Hope Floats* is a wonderfully concise treatise on the nature of hope. When everything else seems as though life is sinking to the depths, hope is buoyant. God's Word is a lifeline of hope when despair comes knocking—and it's not just the kind of hope that crosses its fingers. It's complete confidence, knowing that God always keeps his Word. "Remember the word unto thy servant, upon which thou hast caused me to hope," said the psalmist. "This is my comfort in my affliction: for thy word hath quickened me" (Psalm 119:49–50).

**We glory in tribulations also: knowing that tribulation worketh patience; And patience, experience; and experience, hope: And hope maketh not ashamed; because the love of God is shed abroad in our hearts by the Holy Ghost which is given unto us.**

*—Romans 5:3–5*

**Have courage for the great sorrows of life and patience for the small ones; and when you have laboriously accomplished your daily task, go to sleep in peace. God is awake.**

*—Victor Hugo*

**He that handleth a matter wisely shall find good: and whoso trusteth in the Lord, happy is he.**

*—Proverbs 16:20*

My trust is in you, God of miracles and surprises, for daily I feel your presence in a dozen ways.

**But I will hope continually, and will yet praise thee more and more.**

*—Psalm 71:14*

I might not be able to praise you with an instrument, Lord, but I can still thank you for your faithfulness. When I'm folding laundry, I can praise you for the clothes on my back. When I'm stuck in traffic, I can praise you for the beautiful scenery around me. When I'm fighting illness, I can praise you for the Spirit you breathed into me. And when the people I love struggle, I can praise you for bringing such wonderful people into my life.

I praise you with all the resources at my disposal, Lord. I know that you treasure the motive of my praise—not the means.

**There is one body, and one Spirit, even as ye are called in one hope of your calling.**

*—Ephesians 4:4*

Today, I long to make a difference—to pass along peace and joy and somehow resurrect hope in weary hearts.

**But, beloved, be not ignorant of this one thing, that one day is with the Lord as a thousand years, and a thousand years as one day.**

*—2 Peter 3:8*

When trouble strikes, O God, small signs of hope found in ordinary places restore us: friends, random kindness, shared pain and support. Help us collect them like mustard seeds that can grow into a spreading harvest of well-being.

**But seek ye first the kingdom of God, and his righteousness; and all these things shall be added unto you.**

*—Matthew 6:33*

**Love the Lord with all your might;**
**Turn to him, seek him day and night.**

*—William Wordsworth, "Peter Bell"*

**In hope of eternal life, which God, that cannot lie, promised before the world began.**

*—Titus 1:2*

This gift of life is precious, and I know my eternity is secure in you. Though my days are not always easy, I know that you stay faithfully by my side—guiding my steps and filling my heart with joy.